THE BOOK OF SEX IN MARRIAGE

A Guide to Healthy and Intimate Relationships

Victoria O Banks

copyright©2023 Victoria O Banks

All Rights Reserved

TABLE OF CONTENTS

INTRODUCTION

CHAPTER ONE

BREAKING THE MYTH OF THE 'NORMAL' MARRIAGE

CHAPTER TWO

COMMUNICATION IS THE KEY

CHAPTER THREE

EXPLORING NEW SEXUAL EXPERIENCES AND FANTASIES

CHAPTER FOUR

EMOTIONAL INTIMACY BEYOND THE BEDROOM

CHAPTER FIVE

NAVIGATING THE CHALLENGES OF LONG-TERM COMMITMENT

CHAPTER SIX

THE IMPORTANCE OF SELF-EXPLORATION

CHAPTER SEVEN

REVITALIZING YOUR SEXUAL RELATIONSHIP

CHAPTER EIGHT

THE POWER OF TOUCH

CHAPTER NINE

EMBRACING VULNERABILITY AND AUTHENTICITY

CONCLUSION

[4]

INTRODUCTION

In a healthy marriage, sex can be an important aspect of intimacy, connection, and physical pleasure. However, maintaining passion and connection in your sexual relationship can be a challenge, especially over the long term. Factors such as busy schedules, conflicting desires, and stress can all take a toll on your sexual relationship. One key to maintaining a fulfilling sexual relationship in marriage is to keep the romance alive. This can include things like planning special date nights, expressing your love and appreciation for each other, and trying new things together. Good communication is also important, as is understanding and respecting each other's desires and boundaries.

Other factors that can contribute to a fulfilling sexual relationship in marriage include practicing intimacy beyond the bedroom, engaging in self-exploration, and seeking out activities that promote intimacy and connection. By making an effort to prioritize and nurture your sexual relationship, you can maintain passion and connection in your marriage.

It is also important to remember that every couple is different, and what works for one couple may not work for another. It is important to communicate openly and honestly with your partner about your desires and needs and to be open to trying new things and experimenting to find what works best for you as a couple. With effort and dedication, you can build a fulfilling and satisfying sexual relationship in your marriage.

The Joy of Sex in Marriage is a book that explores the role of intimacy and sexual pleasure in committed relationships. Written by a relationship expert, this book aims to help couples reignite the passion and connection in their marriage.

The book addresses common misconceptions about sex and marriage and the ways in which society often pressures couples to conform to certain expectations about sexual frequency and behavior. These expectations can often be harmful, leading to frustration and disconnection rather than joy and satisfaction.

Instead, The Joy of Sex in Marriage encourages couples to prioritize their own pleasure and desires and to openly communicate with one another about what they want and need in the bedroom. The book offers practical advice on how to initiate and maintain open, honest communication about sex, as well as how to explore new sexual experiences and fantasies in a safe and consensual way.

In addition to addressing the physical aspects of sex, The Joy of Sex in Marriage also explores the emotional and psychological elements of intimacy, the importance of emotional connection and vulnerability in building a strong, healthy sexual relationship, and offers strategies for navigating the ups and downs of long-term commitment.

Overall, The Joy of Sex in Marriage is a comprehensive guide to fostering deeper connection, intimacy, and pleasure in a committed relationship.

One of the key themes of this book is the importance of open and honest communication. The author says that couples who are able to talk openly and honestly about their sexual desires and boundaries are more likely to have fulfilling, satisfying relationships.

In addition to addressing the physical aspects of sex, I also explore the emotional and psychological elements of intimacy, the importance of emotional connection and vulnerability in building a strong, healthy sexual relationship, and offer strategies for navigating the ups and downs of long-term commitment.

Overall, The Joy of Sex in Marriage is a comprehensive guide to fostering deeper connection, intimacy, and pleasure in a committed relationship. This book offers valuable insights and practical advice for couples of all ages and stages.

In the modern world, sex and relationships can often seem complicated and overwhelming. From societal expectations and media portrayals to the demands of work and family life, it can be easy to lose sight of the joy and pleasure that sex can bring. This book helps couples navigate these challenges and reclaim the intimacy and connection that is vital to a happy, healthy relationship. Despite what many people believe, sex and intimacy do not have to fade over time in a long-term relationship. The Joy of Sex in Marriage shows couples how to reignite the passion and connection in their marriage, and offers practical advice on how to explore new sexual experiences and fantasies in a safe and consensual way.

One of the keys to a fulfilling sexual relationship is understanding and prioritizing your own desires and boundaries. The Joy of Sex in a Marriage encourages couples to communicate openly and honestly about what they want and need in the bedroom, and offers strategies for initiating and maintaining this type of open communication.

In addition to addressing the physical aspects

of sex, I also talk about the emotional and psychological elements of intimacy, the importance of emotional connection and vulnerability in building a strong, healthy sexual relationship, and offer strategies for navigating the ups and downs of long-term commitment.

CHAPTER ONE

BREAKING THE MYTH OF THE 'NORMAL' MARRIAGE

In this chapter, we will be discussing the damaging effects of societal expectations on couples' sexual relationships. Many people believe that there is a "normal" way that a sexual relationship should look in a marriage — a certain frequency of sex, specific positions or acts, and so on. However, this simply is not the case. Every couple has its own peculiarity, and what is practicable by one couple may not be practicable by another.

Unfortunately, societal expectations can be harmful to couples' sexual relationships. They can create pressure to conform to certain standards, leading to frustration and disappointment when a couple is unable or unwilling to meet those standards. This pressure can also lead to feelings of inadequacy and failure, causing couples to feel like they are "doing something wrong" if their sex life doesn't look like what they believe it should.

It is important for couples to reject these harmful societal expectations and focus on their own pleasure and desires. This means openly communicating with one another about what they want and need in the bedroom, and not feeling like they have to meet any certain standard or frequency of sex. It also means exploring new sexual experiences and fantasies in a safe and consensual way, and not being afraid to try new things or be vulnerable with one another.

By breaking the myth of the "normal" marriage and prioritizing their own pleasure, couples can create a sexual relationship that is fulfilling and satisfying for both partners. So, it is very important to break the myth of the "normal" marriage and prioritize your own pleasure in order to have a fulfilling and satisfying sexual relationship in your marriage.

One of the biggest myths about sexual relationships in a marriage is that sex should be a certain way – that it should be frequent, passionate, and always enjoyable. This myth can create a lot of pressure for couples, who may feel like they are failing if their sex life doesn't look like what they believe it should. However, the truth is that sex and intimacy in a marriage can take many different forms, and what works for one couple may not work for another.

It is important for couples to remember that there is no "normal" when it comes to sex and intimacy in a marriage. Every couple is unique, with their own desires, boundaries, and needs. By rejecting society's expectations and focusing on their own pleasure and desires, couples can create a sexual relationship that is fulfilling and satisfying for both partners.

This means openly communicating with one another about what they want and need in the bedroom, and not feeling like they have to meet any certain standard or frequency of sex. It also means exploring new sexual experiences and fantasies in a safe and consensual way, and not being afraid to try new things or be vulnerable with one another.

In addition to prioritizing their own pleasure, it is also important for couples to focus on emotional intimacy and connection. This means being open and vulnerable with one another, and creating a safe and supportive environment where they can share their thoughts, feelings, and desires. By fostering emotional intimacy and connection, couples can build a stronger, healthier sexual relationship that is based on trust, respect, and mutual understanding.

Another myth about sexual relationships in a marriage is that sex should always be passionate and spontaneous. While there is certainly nothing wrong with passionate, spontaneous sex, it is important for couples to remember that this is not the only way to have a fulfilling and satisfying sexual relationship. In fact, some couples may find that their sex life is more fulfilling when it is planned and intentional, rather than spontaneous.

It is important for couples to find what works for them, and to remember that there is no "right" or "wrong" way to have sex. By openly communicating with one another about their desires and boundaries, couples can create a sexual relationship that is fulfilling and satisfying for both partners. This means being open to trying new things and exploring new sexual experiences and fantasies safely and consensual way.

It is also important for couples to remember that a fulfilling and satisfying sexual relationship takes work and effort. It is normal for couples to experience ups and downs, and there will be times when one partner may be more interested in sex than the other. It is important for couples to communicate openly and honestly about their desires and boundaries, and to be patient and understanding with one another.

In the following chapters, we will delve further into the importance of open and honest communication, exploring new sexual experiences and fantasies, and fostering emotional intimacy and connection in a committed relationship. So, it is very important to break the myth of the "normal" marriage and prioritize your own pleasure in order to have a fulfilling and satisfying sexual relationship in your marriage.

CHAPTER TWO
COMMUNICATION IS THE KEY

In this chapter, we will be discussing the importance of open and honest communication in a sexual relationship. Communication is key to any relationship, and this is especially true when it comes to sex and intimacy. By openly communicating with your partner about your desires, boundaries, and needs, you can create a sexual relationship that is fulfilling and satisfying for both of you.

However, many couples struggle with open and honest communication about sex and intimacy. This can be due to a variety of reasons, such as fear of rejection, embarrassment, or simply not knowing how to bring up the topic, and this can lead to frustration, disappointment, and a lack of connection in the relationship. It is important for couples to recognize that these are normal and natural feelings, and to work together to overcome them.

One of the keys to effective communication about sex and intimacy is creating a safe and supportive environment where you can talk openly and honestly with your partner. This means setting aside time to have these conversations and making sure that you are both in a calm and receptive state of mind. It is also important to remember to listen to your partner and try to understand their perspective, even if you don't agree with them.

One way to facilitate effective communication about sex and intimacy is to set aside dedicated time to talk about these topics. This might mean scheduling regular "check-ins" where you can talk openly and honestly with your partner about your sexual relationship. It is also helpful to set aside time to talk about specific issues or concerns as they arise.

Another key to effective communication is using "I" statements, rather than "you" statements. This means expressing your own feelings and needs, rather than accusing your partner of doing something wrong. For example, rather than saying 'you never initiate intimacy say that 'I am the only one doing that and I would like the two of you to be involved in the initiation of sex. This approach will bring a positive result than confrontation.

Effective communication about sex and intimacy is not just about discussing your desires and boundaries, but also about actively listening to your partner and trying to understand their perspective. It is important to remember that both partners have a role to play in the sexual relationship and that each person's needs and desires are equally important.

It is also important to be patient and understanding with one another when it comes to communication about sex and intimacy. This means being willing to have difficult conversations and working together to find solutions to any challenges or issues that may arise. It is equally important to remember that it can take time to build trust and establish open and honest communication in a sexual relationship and that it is normal to have disagreements in the process.

Effective communication is essential to any relationship, and this is especially true when it comes to sex and intimacy. By openly and honestly communicating with your partner about your desires, boundaries, and needs, you can create a sexual relationship that is fulfilling and satisfying for both of you.
One key to effective communication about sex and intimacy is creating a safe and supportive environment where you can talk openly and honestly with your partner. This means setting aside dedicated time to have these conversations and making sure that you are both in a calm and receptive state of mind. It is also important to choose a location that is private and free from distractions, as this will

help you both to focus on the conversation. Effective communication about sex and intimacy is an ongoing process that requires effort and commitment from both partners. It is important to remember that every couple has its peculiarity and what pleases one couple may not please another. It is also important to be open to trying new things and exploring new sexual experiences and fantasies safely and consensually.

It is also important to be patient and understanding with one another when it comes to communication about sex and intimacy. This means being willing to have difficult conversations and work

In the following chapters, we will delve further into the importance of open and honest communication, exploring new sexual experiences and fantasies, and fostering emotional intimacy and connection in a committed relationship. So, it is very important to communicate openly and honestly with your partner about sex and intimacy in order to have a fulfilling and satisfying sexual relationship in your marriage.

CHAPTER THREE
EXPLORING NEW SEXUAL EXPERIENCES AND FANTASIES

In this chapter, we will be discussing the importance of exploring new sexual experiences and fantasies in a committed relationship. Many couples find that their sex life becomes stale or routine over time and that they are no longer as interested in sex as they once were. This is completely normal, and there are many ways that couples can reignite the spark and keep their sex life exciting and fulfilling.

One way to do this is by exploring new sexual experiences and fantasies together. This can be as simple as trying out new positions or incorporating new toys or accessories into your sex life, or it can be more involved, such as exploring role-playing like exchanging the positioning of the two of you, doing it in the bathroom or on the couch Whatever your interests and desires, it is important to approach the exploration of new sexual experiences and fantasies with an open and curious mindset.

However, it is also important to remember that the exploration of new sexual experiences and fantasies should always be consensual and respectful. This means having open and honest communication with your partner about your desires and boundaries and making sure that you both feel comfortable and safe. It is also important to remember to use safe sex practices.

One key to exploring new sexual experiences and fantasies is open and honest communication with your partner. By discussing your desires and boundaries, and actively listening to your partner's thoughts and feelings, you can create a safe and supportive environment where you can both feel comfortable trying new things.

It is also important to remember that not all sexual experiences and fantasies are right for everyone, and that it is okay to have different preferences and boundaries. It is important to respect your partner's boundaries to communicate openly and honestly about what you are and are not comfortable with and to be patient and understanding with one another.

Another key to exploring new sexual experiences and fantasies is to approach them with an open and curious mindset. This means being open to trying new things, and not being afraid to be vulnerable with your partner.

Exploring new sexual experiences and fantasies can be a fun and exciting way to bring excitement and passion back into a relationship. However, it is important to approach this exploration in a safe and consensual way. This means openly communicating with your partner about your desires and boundaries, and respecting your partner's boundaries as well.

One way to explore new sexual experiences and fantasies is to start small and build up gradually. This might mean trying a new position or technique, or introducing a new toy or prop into your bedroom play. It is important to be open and curious and to approach these new experiences with an open and positive mindset.

Another way to explore new sexual experiences and fantasies is to talk about them with your partner. This might mean sharing your own fantasies or desires or asking your partner about theirs. By being open and honest with one another, you can create a safe and supportive environment where you can both feel comfortable trying new things.

In the following chapters, we will delve into exploring new sexual experiences and fantasies, and fostering emotional intimacy and connection in a committed relationship. So, it is very important to explore new sexual experiences and fantasies in a safe and consensual way in order to have a fulfilling and satisfying sexual relationship in your marriage.

Exploring new sexual experiences and fantasies can be a fun and exciting way to bring excitement and passion back into a relationship. However, it is important to approach this exploration in a safe and consensual way. This means openly communicating with your partner about your desires and boundaries, and respecting your partner's boundaries as well.

One way to explore new sexual experiences and fantasies is to start small and build up gradually. This might mean trying a new position or technique, or introducing a new toy or prop into your bedroom play. It is important to be open and curious and to approach these new experiences with an open and positive mindset.

Another way to explore new sexual experiences and fantasies is to do some research and reading together. There are many books, articles, and resources available that can help couples to explore new sexual experiences and fantasies in a safe and consensual way. By doing research and reading together, couples can learn about new techniques, positions, and practices that they may be interested in trying.

So, it is very important to explore new sexual experiences and fantasies in a safe and consensual way in order to have a fulfilling and satisfying sexual relationship in your marriage.

CHAPTER FOUR
EMOTIONAL INTIMACY BEYOND THE BEDROOM

Emotional intimacy is an important aspect of a fulfilling sexual relationship. It involves a deep connection and understanding between partners, and a willingness to be vulnerable and open with each other.

Here are some key points to consider when thinking about the role of emotional intimacy in a sexual relationship:

Connection: A strong emotional connection between partners can enhance intimacy and create a sense of closeness and attachment. This connection is built through consistent communication, trust, and support for one another.

Vulnerability: Allowing oneself to be vulnerable and open with a partner can create a deeper level of intimacy. This means being willing to share your thoughts, feelings, and desires with your partner, and being open to hearing their thoughts and feelings as well.

Communication: Effective communication is essential for creating and maintaining emotional intimacy. This means openly and honestly sharing your needs, boundaries, and desires with your partner, and actively listening to and understanding their perspective.

Trust: Trust is a key component of emotional intimacy. It involves being honest and transparent with your partner and being there for them when they need support or guidance.

Support: Showing support for your partner's goals, dreams, and aspirations can strengthen the emotional bond between you. This can involve being understanding and empathetic when they face challenges, and celebrating their accomplishments.

Respect: Showing respect for your partner's feelings, boundaries, and desires is essential for building and maintaining emotional intimacy. This means valuing their perspective and being considerate of their needs.

Empathy: Being able to understand and share your partner's emotions can help create a deeper emotional connection. This involves being able to put yourself in their shoes and feeling what they are feeling.

Shared experiences: Engaging in shared experiences and activities can help build emotional intimacy. This can include anything from shared hobbies and interests to exploring new things together and trying new things.

Physical intimacy: Physical intimacy, such as touch and affection, can also play a role in building emotional intimacy. Physical touch can help create a sense of closeness and connection and can strengthen the emotional bond between partners.

Time and effort: Building emotional intimacy takes time and effort. It involves consistently communicating, showing support, and being there for your partner. By making the effort to prioritize emotional intimacy, you can create a strong, fulfilling relationship with your partner.

Safety: Feeling safe and secure in the relationship is important for emotional intimacy. This means feeling free to express your thoughts, feelings, and desires without fear of judgment or rejection.

Intentionality: Making a conscious effort to prioritize emotional intimacy can help strengthen the bond between partners. This might involve setting aside dedicated time for deep conversations, making an effort to understand your partner's perspective, or regularly expressing appreciation and support for one another.

Self-awareness: Being self-aware and in touch with your own emotions is important for building emotional intimacy with your partner. This means being able to recognize and express your own feelings, and being open to hearing and understanding your partner's feelings as well.

Flexibility: Being flexible and open to change can help build emotional intimacy. This might involve being open to trying new things, learning from one another, and adapting to each other's needs and desires.

Commitment: Making a commitment to building and maintaining emotional intimacy can help create a strong, fulfilling relationship with your partner. This might involve making a commitment to regularly communicate, show support, and be there for one another.

Overall, emotional intimacy is an important aspect of a fulfilling sexual relationship. It involves a deep connection, vulnerability, and strong communication and trust. By prioritizing safety, intentionality, self-awareness, flexibility, and commitment, you can create a strong, fulfilling relationship with your partner.

CHAPTER FIVE

NAVIGATING THE CHALLENGES OF LONG-TERM COMMITMENT

Maintaining passion and connection in a long-term commitment, such as a marriage, can be a challenge for many couples. Couples that want to navigate this challenge need to put some techniques in their marriage to make it more interesting.

Communication: Good communication is key to maintaining a strong connection with your partner. Make sure to regularly check in with each other about your feelings, needs, and expectations.

Quality time: Create time for each other, and do things that interest you both. This will make you more connected and strengthen your relationship

Romance: Keep the romance alive by

planning special date nights, surprising each other with small gestures, and expressing your love and appreciation for one another.

Flexibility: Be open to change and try new things. This can help keep things interesting and prevent boredom or stagnation in the relationship.

Respect: Show your partner respect by listening to them, valuing their opinions, and showing appreciation for their efforts.

Emotional intelligence: Work on understanding and managing your own emotions, as well as those of your partner. This can help improve communication and reduce conflict in the relationship.

Seek support: If you are struggling to maintain passion and connection in your marriage, consider seeking the help of a therapist or counselor. They may provide valuable tips and solutions.

Nurture your friendship: In addition to being romantic partners, it's important to also be good friends with your spouse. Spend time doing things that you enjoy together, have meaningful conversations, and support each other in your individual interests and pursuits.

Practice gratitude: Expressing gratitude towards your partner can help strengthen your connection and improve your overall happiness. Make an effort to regularly thank your partner for the things they do for you and the positive impact they have on your life.

Set aside alone time: It's important to have time for yourself and to pursue your own interests. Encourage your partner to do the same, and make sure to respect each other's need for alone time.

Keep the physical connection strong: Physical intimacy is an important aspect of any relationship, and it's important to make time for it even in long-term commitments. Make an effort to maintain a strong physical connection with your partner through things like cuddling, holding hands, kissing, and regular intimacy.

Manage conflict effectively: Conflict is a normal part of any relationship, but it's important to learn how to manage it effectively. Try to stay calm and communicate openly and honestly with your partner. Seek the help of a therapist or counselor if needed.

Seek new experiences: Trying new things and experiencing new things together can help keep the passion and excitement alive in your relationship. Consider taking up a new hobby or activity together, or planning a vacation to a new destination.

Add surprises to your relationship: Let your relationship be full of surprises. Surprise your partner with small gestures, plan special date nights, and make an effort to show your love and appreciation for them regularly.

Keep the spark alive: It's natural for the initial excitement and passion of a new relationship to fade over time, but it's important to make an effort to keep the spark alive in a long-term commitment. Try new things together, surprise each other, and keep the romance alive by doing things like planning special date nights and expressing your love and appreciation for one another. Do not allow stress or your career to destroy the reason for your relationship. Let the attraction keep on blossoming

Make time for each other: In today's busy world, it can be easy to let other commitments and responsibilities take precedence over your relationship. Make an effort to set aside quality time for each other and prioritize your relationship.

Practice forgiveness: It's inevitable that you and your partner will make mistakes or hurt each other's feelings at some point. It's important to practice forgiveness and move on from conflicts rather than dwelling on them. This can help strengthen your bond and improve your overall relationship satisfaction.

Practice good communication: Every good relationship practices great communication Make sure to regularly check in with each other about your feelings, needs, and expectations. Practice active listening and be open and honest with your partner.

Take care of yourself: In order to be able to give your best to your relationship, it's important to also take care of yourself. Make sure to prioritize your own well-being, including your physical and mental health.

Be open to change: Relationships are dynamic and can change over time. It's important to be open to change and adapt to the evolving needs of your relationship. This can help keep things interesting and prevent boredom or stagnation. If you need to put on better action to make your relationship interesting, it is better to do so as it is difficult to get a better result with the same habit. A new habit or attitude brings a new result. Remember, maintaining passion and connection in a long-term commitment requires effort and dedication from both partners. By making an effort to keep the spark alive, make time for each other, practice forgiveness, communicate effectively, take care of yourself, be open to change, making an effort to nurture your friendship, practice gratitude, set aside alone time, maintain a strong physical connection, manage conflict effectively, seek new experiences, and keep the romance alive, you can strengthen your bond and build a healthy, fulfilling relationship.

[42]

CHAPTER SIX
THE IMPORTANCE OF SELF-EXPLORATION

Self-exploration is the process of learning more about yourself and understanding your own desires, values, and needs. It is an important aspect of personal growth and development and can be particularly beneficial in a relationship. There are many ways to engage in self-exploration, such as through journaling, therapy, meditation, or taking part in activities that allow you to explore your interests and passions. Whatever method you choose, the key is to be open and honest with yourself and to be willing to embrace change and growth. By making self-exploration a priority, you can gain a deeper understanding of yourself and build a more fulfilling and satisfying life.

Improved self-awareness: By engaging in self-exploration, you can gain a deeper understanding of your own thoughts, feelings, and behaviors. This can help you become more self-aware and better able to identify and address any personal issues or challenges.

Increased self-esteem: When you understand and prioritize your own desires, you are more likely to feel confident and self-assured, and this will increase your self-worth and self-esteem

Enhanced relationships: When you are self-aware and confident in your own desires and needs, you are better equipped to communicate openly and honestly with your partner.

Improved decision-making: By understanding your own values and priorities, you can make more informed and confident decisions that align with your personal goals and desires.

Greater overall satisfaction: By

understanding and prioritizing your own desires, you are more likely to feel fulfilled and satisfied in all aspects of your life.

Improved communication with others: By understanding your own desires and needs, you are better equipped to communicate openly and honestly with others. This can lead to more fulfilling and satisfying relationships with friends, family, and romantic partners.

Greater personal growth: Engaging in self-exploration can help you identify areas of your life that you would like to work on or change. By focusing on personal growth, you can become a happier and more fulfilled person.

Increased self-acceptance: As you learn more about yourself through self-exploration, you may come to understand and accept aspects of yourself that you previously struggled with. This can lead to greater self-acceptance and a more positive self-image.

Enhanced emotional intelligence: Engaging in self-exploration can help you become more self-aware, which can in turn improve your emotional intelligence. This means that you will be better able to recognize and manage your own emotions, as well as those of others.

Greater overall happiness: By understanding and prioritizing your own desires and needs, you are more likely to feel fulfilled and satisfied in all aspects of your life. This can lead to increased overall happiness and well-being.

Reflect on your thoughts and feelings: Take time to think about your own thoughts, feelings, and motivations. This can help you gain a deeper understanding of yourself and your desires.

Seek feedback from others: Ask friends, family, or a therapist for their honest feedback on your strengths, weaknesses, and areas for growth. This can provide valuable insights and help you identify areas for self-improvement.

Explore your values and beliefs: Consider what values and beliefs are most important to you and how they shape your decisions and actions. This can help you understand what truly matters to you and what you want to prioritize in your life.

Take part in activities that allow you to explore your interests and passions: Engaging in activities that you enjoy and that allow you to explore your interests and passions can help you learn more about yourself and what brings you joy and fulfillment.

Remember, self-exploration is a journey of personal growth and development. It requires effort and dedication, but the benefits can be significant. By reflecting on your thoughts and feelings, seeking feedback from others, exploring your values and beliefs, taking part in activities that allow you to explore your interests and passions, and seeking support if needed, you can gain a deeper understanding of yourself and build a more fulfilling and satisfying relationship with your spouse or partner.

CHAPTER SEVEN
REVITALIZING YOUR SEXUAL RELATIONSHIP

On the off chance that you are coupled and trapped in a hopeless cycle, you're in good company. Even though relationship dry spells are normal, it doesn't help couples who are going through one. The sex drive dies when we become used to someone, and the more we get used to them, the less exciting sex becomes.

This doesn't mean that every long-term couple has problems in the bedroom; in fact, there is a lot of research that says people can stay very in love for a long time. However, research suggests that couples who engage in particular sexual behaviors tend to be happier with their sexual lives. Also, regardless of whether you're as of now fulfilled, investing energy into your sexual coexistence and learning new things will help your sexual coexistence.

It is common for the intensity and frequency of sexual activity to decrease over time in a long-term commitment, but this doesn't have to be a permanent state of affairs. Remember, revitalizing your sexual relationship requires effort and dedication from both partners. By communicating openly and honestly, seeking new experiences, setting aside quality time, practicing physical affection, taking care of yourself, and seeking support if needed, you can rekindle the spark in your marriage and build a healthy, fulfilling sexual relationship. If you don't have a sex life, here are some quick hints I've tried to get you back on track.

Seek new experiences: Trying new things in the bedroom can help to keep things interesting and rekindle the spark. This can include things like introducing new positions, trying out different types of foreplay, or using toys or other enhancements.

Set aside quality time: In today's busy world, it can be easy to let other commitments and responsibilities take precedence over your relationship. Make an effort to set aside quality time for each other and prioritize your sexual relationship.

Practice mindfulness: Being present and fully engaged in a moment can help to enhance the intimacy and pleasure of the sexual activity. Consider incorporating mindfulness practices, such as meditation or focused breathing, into your sexual encounters.

Experiment with different types of touch: Touch is an important aspect of sexual intimacy. Experiment with different types of touch, such as light or firm, and pay attention to your partner's responses to find out what they enjoy.

Explore fantasies and desires: Discussing and exploring each other's fantasies and desires can be a fun and exciting way to bring novelty and excitement into your sexual encounters.

Practice good communication: Good communication is key to any healthy relationship, including in matters of sexuality. Make sure to discuss your desires, needs, and any concerns you may have with your partner.

Make an effort to keep the romance alive: The romance and passion of a new relationship can fade over time, but it's important to make an effort to keep the spark alive in a long-term commitment. Try new things together, surprise each other, and keep the romance alive by doing things like planning special date nights and expressing your love and appreciation for one another.

Practice good self-care: Taking care of yourself can help you feel more confident and satisfied in your sexual relationship. Make sure to prioritize your own well-being, including your physical and mental health, and engage in activities that nourish and rejuvenate you.

Make an effort to connect outside of the bedroom: It's important to build and maintain a strong emotional connection with your partner, as this can enhance intimacy in the bedroom. Make time for non-sexual activities that allow you to connect and bond with your partners such as going on a date or participating in a shared hobby or activity.

Be open to trying new things: Experimenting with new positions, locations, and activities can help to keep things interesting and bring novelty and excitement into your sexual encounters.

Show appreciation and affection: Show your partner that you appreciate and care for them by expressing your love and affection for them through words and actions. This can include things like saying "I love you," giving compliments, and performing small acts of kindness.

Practice good communication: Good communication is key to any healthy relationship, including in matters of sexuality. Make sure to discuss your desires, needs, and any concerns you may have with your partner.

Set up a sex "fact-finding" night.
Spend one night having a candid conversation about what sexual things you like and don't like, trying out new sex moves, and talking about your hidden fantasies. Try not to compel yourself to be provocative, simply investigate to see what you like and express out loud whatever you typically abstain from expressing out of dread of humiliating yourself or sounding coldhearted."

According to the findings of the study, people between the ages of 18 and 25 have very different sexual expectations. Couples must communicate their preferences in bed in order to have a mutually enjoyable experience because these expectations are unlikely to change overnight.

Take a couples' sex class and practice during the weekend.
A whole new idea of sex play will be opened up when you take a sex class in a fun, not intimidating learning environment, couples can learn about new sex positions, techniques, and toys and props for sex play.

Whether or not to go on a sexy overnight getaway, try a little role-playing. Makeup histories for your characters somewhat early, spruce up and play around with it, the couples that move together have better sexual experiences.
Yet, a few couples working their direction back to closeness might find a provocative meeting testing. Going on a romantic getaway can put too much pressure on one's performance. There are so many benefits to enjoy when spending time together without sex. Together, go hiking or explore a new area.

Enjoy yourself in front of your partner
Masturbating allows your partner to see you enjoying pleasure, which can build intimacy. Allowing your partner to observe how and where you prefer to be touched is practicing a level of vulnerability that fosters intimacy. Additionally, masturbation has many positive effects on one's health, such as elevating one's mood and releasing accumulated stress, both of which are great preparations for more sex.

Have a one-on-one conversation to get your concerns out of the air.
In many relationships, sex droughts are caused by a lack of communication. A recent study found that couples who frequently disagreed were ten times happier than those who avoided conflict. Practice having difficult conversations. Sometimes, having a conversation you've been avoiding is all it takes to cultivate intimacy.
Don't let your partner's words discourage you. Just keep in mind that part of trying to

improve your relationship is figuring out what's wrong. If you are willing to make concessions, there are solutions. You can come up with solutions to injustices even if you are sexually mismatched.

Tap into your inner needs if nothing else works.
Stress and life's busyness are other factors that affect sexual intimacy, but there are productive ways to overcome obstacles. No matter how many dozens of chill nights you and your long-term partner have shared, there is something that keeps you tuning in for more. Sometimes all it takes to get back on track is to tap into something simple, but many people let fear or embarrassment stop them from trying. However, just as people age and change over time, so does your sexual life: It's possible that the feeling that piqued your interest when you first met is different now.
The way into a cheerful, satisfying sexual coexistence with a drawn-out darling is by switching things around and making your

own new sex "rules" as you come. However, these "rules" aren't set in stone, and they change over time; They change and grow alongside your relationship. Your sexual life can change in tandem with your ever-changing partnership, just as a causal relationship may progress to commitment.

Everything is wonderful and carefree at first, and it's easy to have sexual feelings for your partner. However, after the wedding, things like children, debt, and boredom, to name a few, can dampen your sex life.

Find porn that you both enjoy.

Talking about porn with your partner can be both illuminating and energizing, regardless of whether you are a novice or a seasoned expert with a curated collection of X-rated videos. And even if you don't think you would like porn, don't forget that there is a lot of variety out there. If you and your partner can get along, you might just have to figure out what works for you.

"Pornography has progressed significantly with regards to variety and quality throughout recent years, and there is a tremendous assortment accessible, going from hot and terrible all-activity to out-and-out realistic movies and, surprisingly, Hollywood-style

Jump into a recent fad of sex

Have a discussion with your accomplice about how you need to integrate more play and assortment into your everyday practice, and afterward challenge yourselves to attempt another position one time each month. You can try a standing position, a position from behind, a side position, a bending down position, or any other position that piques your interest.

Don't waste your time. Hear us out: In a long-term relationship, a lot of what makes sex so erotic and fun are how well you know each other, how much you care about each other, and how willing you are to invest in the other person's pleasure. However, you may miss out on a lot of the fun if you get into the habit of only having quickies before bed or work.

Sex is about being intimate and feeling connected to your partner. Quickies and low-key sex can be fun at times, but more prolonged sex can pay off big in terms of intimacy and pleasure.

Make time for both of you to connect, and work on fighting more fairly.

The hotness of makeup sex can be attested to by a lot of people. However, avoid using sex as the sole means of resolving disagreements. After you have resolved any issues, it ought to be more of a celebration. On the other hand, fighting can cause some couples to go a long time without having sex, which is also bad. In order to maintain a healthy relationship and prevent conflict from becoming a symptom, the advice here is to develop strong conflict-resolution skills.

Establish a sex menu.

When you are in a drawn-out relationship, particularly when you cohabitate, quite possibly of the most widely recognized text you'll shoot each other's way would it be a good idea for us to have for supper? So, if you want to keep things interesting, think about a different kind of menu.

Three sexual acts that each partner would like to perform as an appetizer, three sexual acts that they would like to perform as a main course, and three sexual acts that they would like to perform as a dessert will be written by each partner. The couple will then negotiate a sex menu for that night by reading each other's menus.

When you're in a long-term relationship, how well you know each other's bodies make sex fun and sometimes unnecessary. You know where to thrust, how to get off each other quickly, and which areas are the most sensitive. That can be entertaining and convenient, but it can also stifle creativity. Therefore, you might want to think about literally writing down what you know and then determining what you can learn by discussing it.

When you are finished, start by touching, licking, and caressing your partner's feet, starting with the left foot, and asking, "Does it feel good when I kiss you there?" Each person takes turns drawing the other person's body as best they can. This is only for your eyes. Does licking you there make you feel good? Do you prefer me to rub your feet more vigorously, or do you prefer me to do so gently?
After that, progress all the way up to your partner's head. Make notes on the drawing as you go to each part of your partner's body.

If you have been together for a long time, you may be surprised to learn that your partner may have changed over time, provided that you have previously noticed their body type and similarity.

Try not to limit the significance of non-sexual touch.
Some of the time, zeroing in on non-erogenous zones can be more sensual than participating in plainly sexual exercises. Besides amping up your everyday contacting — which studies recommend can assist with supporting general relationship and accomplice fulfillment — consider a non-sexual movement that actually requires contact, similar to a back rub, you can purchase rub oils and setting the state of mind by switching out the lights, lighting candles, and getting totally bare.

Take as much time as necessary scouring and kneading your accomplice, and get as near your accomplice's privates as you would like, however, don't contact."
After you each have spent a little while rubbing one another, you can partake in some dangerous sex.

Change around the timing.

You and your accomplice may be evening people who get turned on before bed or morning individuals who are firing up to go when you awaken. Be that as it may, with an end goal to keep your sexual coexistence amazing and drawing in, change around the planning of your lovemaking.

On the off chance that you're accustomed to having it on those very days in view of timetable comfort, take a stab at having a fast in and out on different days when you could have less time; in the event that you generally engage in sexual relations around evening time, attempt it in the first part of the day. The oddity of accomplishing something else carries with it a specific degree of energy.

Quit playing the "you need to start" game.

Assuming you're still mostly certain,

hopefully not by mistake, that your accomplice needs to take the primary action or that the next move is consistently up to you, you want to step beyond your particular safe places.

Put your longings out there and show your accomplice that you think that they are appealing and hot, Individuals fall into schedules and assumptions for who ought to start, so realizing your accomplice is turned on and needs to be with you is a turn-on all by itself.

Compromise playing "provider" and "beneficiary."

Assuming that one of you is substantially more of a provider than the other and that it worked for your relationship, marvelous. Yet, that doesn't imply that changing around those jobs occasionally, is an ill-conceived notion, particularly assuming that you make it an exceptional, suggestive experience.

Conclude what job each will 'play' for the evening, and afterward have another night where you turn around the jobs, Frequently, individuals become involved with the jobs they play in bed, as well as the assumptions they think their accomplice has of them. That can make impedance as far as having the option to surrender oneself to finish unwinding and joy.

Trade the Nightgown for something hotter one time per month.
Your accomplice might believe you're similarly as hot in your school sweats as you are when decked out for a dark tie undertaking, yet that doesn't mean they will not see the value in a little startling exertion as a hot nightie or even another set of clothing.

There's a certain joy to be acquired from getting some margin to dress for sex, Feel provocative in the thing you're putting on, and permit your accomplice the valuable chance to be outwardly turned on by the thing you're wearing."

Attempt another non-sexual leisure activity together.

Regardless of whether you're by and large blissful in your relationship, you could run into a timeframe when you don't feel as turned on or associated — and that is exceptionally normal and thoroughly OK. Attempt to participate in exercises that revitalize the synthetic substances related to new and enthusiastic love: chemicals like dopamine, adrenaline, and serotonin.

One method for reigniting the flash is to accomplish something nonsexual together that causes you to feel more eager to hop once again into bed when you're finished. Like parting ways so you become inquisitive about each other's lives beyond the relationship. Oddity, secret, and tension filled your association in the good old days, so you really

[67]

want to reproduce a comparable climate to reignite the enthusiasm,

Assume a sense of ownership with your own sexual craving.

Regardless of whether your accomplice is awesome at preparing you excited and to go, it's not only dependent upon them and how they manage their hands, privates, and mouths to set you up for intercourse. sexual longing doesn't generally fall into place, and it really depends on you to make it for yourself. Your accomplice can assume a part in this, yet don't generally place the obligation in their court.

Large numbers of us aren't in that frame of mind for sex until after we're turned on, so don't hold on until you're in that frame of mind — put yourself in that frame of mind. Fantasize, read a sensual story, watch pornography, be a tease. Effectively get turned on, and afterward, check whether you're in that frame of mind."

[68]

All things considered, there's not a great explanation to compel yourself to constantly be in that frame of mind or need to sex a specific number of times each week, a month, and so forth. Pay attention to your instinct and track down the equilibrium that works for you.

Put sex on the plan — in a real sense.

Putting sex on your schedules and agenda can add expectation and fabricate expectation. You can call the update anything you desire, however putting forth the attempt to put it on your schedules reminds you to focus on it.

As your lives get more occupied, it turns out to be not difficult to set sex aside for later. The issue is, the point at which you do that for a really long time, you might find yourself or your accomplice feeling disengaged and out of nowhere acknowledge you have some significant relationship issues to work out. Focus on engaging in sexual relations a specific number of times each week or each month, and finish it, regardless of how occupied or how tired you are.

Up your sexting game.
Rather than just utilizing your messaging discussions to refresh each other about the occasion in your home or work environment, make your texts a little kinkier once in a while and bother for what's to come later in the day.

Portray what you are wearing in bed and how you are contacting yourself considering them. You can push this game along over the course of the day, and when your accomplice gets back that night, flashes will fly.

Remove it from the room.
At the point when the mindset strikes, you probably won't be in your room, candles lit and it is totally generally alluring to feel you. You might be sweat-soaked from the rec center or strolling in from an energy-sapping workday when you get a brief look at your

accomplice sitting on the lounge chair or mixing pureed tomatoes, and you unexpectedly need to have sex with them, surrender to those motivations and don't stress over having intercourse on the love seat or the kitchen counter that far are the only ones at home. Sex doesn't need to be some ideal room circumstance. Trust your longings and accept circumstances for what they are.

Have furious sex

Assuming your folks generally advised you to never head to sleep furious, you should make a special case with your accomplice. Since, as certain individuals definitely know, furious sex can be incredibly hot.
The piece of the mind that is set off with outrage is a similar part set off during sex. Along these lines, it's normal to need sex when irate, regardless of whether you haven't made up. Besides, during this second, you could zero in somewhat more on yourself, which is additionally OK.

Plan an excursion for sex.
Regardless of whether you're hitched and you're putting something aside for an outing with the children, focus on time together, particularly time away from ordinary burdens and obligations. An excursion wherein your main arrangement is to get it on constantly — will re-energize your sexual coexistence.
Book a pleasant lodge in the forest or a lavish lodging for the end of the week. Pack your most loved toys and hot outfits — or no outfits by any means — leave your telephones and different gadgets off, and partake in the time with your accomplice.

Discuss each other's sexual dreams

Rather than getting into bed and understanding books or looking at Instagram consistently, permit your pre-sleep time routine to incorporate examining dreams every once in a while.
In long-haul connections, particularly, you could move away from how your accomplice's

desires advance after some time, and getting some information about them can bring you closer.

Try not to pick little fights that influence your sexual coexistence.
Regardless of how viable you are with somebody; you will undoubtedly find minor disturbances that rankle you in the relationship. Accordingly, picking your fights carefully will guarantee you keep the sentiment in your sexual coexistence alive. Assuming that somebody left the carport entryway open once more and this upsets you, simply close it and let it go. I'm certain that there are seemingly insignificant details that irritated them too. Calling attention to those seemingly insignificant details constantly, rather than simply managing them, can cause a greater number of battles than not perspiring it and doing it without anyone's help.

Permit your accomplice to direct your development.
Part of being in a drawn-out relationship is

fostering an earnest degree of trust. Similarly, if you realize your accomplice will be consistent with their promise, you ought to have the option to believe how they guide you in the room. Couples in a committed, long-haul relationship ought to play what is known as the mirror game.

In this "game," you or your accomplice can get going as the pioneer and you exhibit the various things that turn you on, and the accomplice must duplicate or mirror your developments. The main catch is that they can't contact you — they can duplicate how you're treating yourself.

You will find that you learn things about one another that, even after numerous years together, are new.

When you've both had turns as the pioneer, you can allow that development to transform into at long last contacting one another.

Practice yoga breathing together.
Specialists trust that a tremendous consider having the option to climax is basically

relaxing. It might sound straightforward, yet for some individuals, it's hard to do this during sex. Yet, working on matching up your breath and making everyone profound and careful, similar to yoga breathing can fabricate the power of your climax.

Behold, sit opposite each other, and take a gander at one another. Notice your accomplice's breathing example. How can it look? Is there an ascent on your accomplice's shoulders? An extension of their chest? Start to carry your breath into a similar musicality. At the point when your breath mood is concurrent, start to contact one another and keep up with coordinated breath through your whole sexual experience."

Have intercourse with your fingertips.

With regard to sexual excitement, the fingertips may simply be the most underestimated body part, their wealth of tangible neurons makes them especially delicate. What's more, in light of the fact that countless couples race through the movements of sex, they can fail to remember that a delicate touch can be the most effective.

Make up your own "rules" — and go ahead and transform them.
In some cases, tossing out the standard book is the most ideal way to re-energize your sexual coexistence. All things considered, there's nobody size-fits-all sex fix for each couple, so doing what works for yourself as well as your partner(s) is what's generally significant.

You basically have to figure out how to be straightforward with yourself and your accomplice,
Try by making your own "rules" with your accomplice and giving them a shot for some time. Also, obviously, remember to check in and perceive how you both feel.

Remember, revitalizing your sexual relationship requires effort and dedication from both partners. By practicing good self-care, making an effort to connect outside of the bedroom, being open to trying new things, showing appreciation and affection, practicing good communication, and seeking support if needed, you can rekindle the spark in your marriage and build a healthy, fulfilling sexual relationship.

Try dancing or yoga to release your body's energy in a new way.

Once you've established a connection with your own body, you can then establish a connection with your partner's body.

According to the findings of the study, couples who are sexually inactive are more likely to experience feelings of sadness and to feel unattractive. Find new ways to move and feel at ease in your body to regain sexual power.

Do something new to rekindle your dopamine.

Doing something new fosters a sense of connection and intimacy. Try something new, like an escape room or a ride at an amusement park, that might either scare you or excite you. Dopamine and other brain chemicals are directly linked to physical attraction and romantic passion, so bonding over a new activity together could help spark arousal. You will create dopamine and replicate the same feelings you had during your honeymoon period.

CHAPTER EIGHT
THE POWER OF TOUCH

Physical affection, such as touch, is an important aspect of any healthy relationship. It can help to strengthen your emotional connection with your partner and improve overall relationship satisfaction. Here are some ways that touch can be used to strengthen your connection:

Practice physical affection regularly: Physical affection doesn't have to be limited to sexual activity. Simple acts like holding hands, cuddling, and hugging can all help to strengthen your physical connection. Make an effort to incorporate physical affection into your daily routine

Use touch to communicate your love and appreciation: Show your partner that you love and appreciate them by expressing your affection through touch. This can include things like giving a hug or a kiss, or holding hands.

Engage in touch during non-sexual activities: Physical affection doesn't have to be limited to the bedroom. Incorporating touch into non-sexual activities, such as watching a movie or going for a walk, can help to strengthen your emotional connection. Seek out touch-based activities: Engaging in touch-based activities, such as massages or couples' yoga, can be a fun and enjoyable way to strengthen your physical connection.

Pay attention to body language: Paying attention to your partner's body language can help you understand their comfort level with touch and what types of touch they enjoy.

Use touch to show support and comfort: Touch can be a powerful way to show your partner that you are there for them and to provide comfort and support. This can be especially important during times of stress or crisis.

Practice non-sexual touch: Physical affection doesn't have to be sexual in nature. Simple acts of affection, such as holding hands or giving a hug, can be just as effective in strengthening your connection.

Experiment with different types of touch: Touch can be a powerful way to communicate love and affection. Experiment with different types of touch, such as light or firm, and pay attention to your partner's responses to find out what they enjoy.

Make touch a priority: In today's busy world, it can be easy to let other commitments and responsibilities take precedence over your relationship. Make an effort to set aside quality time for each other and prioritize physical affection.

Practice touch during conflict: Touch can be a powerful tool for de-escalating conflict and promoting a sense of calm and connection. Consider using touch, such as holding hands or cuddling, during times of disagreement to help restore a sense of harmony and intimacy.

Use touch to show appreciation and gratitude: Show your partner that you appreciate and value them by expressing your gratitude through touch. This can include things like giving a hug or a kiss, or holding hands.

Incorporate touch into your daily routine: Physical affection doesn't have to be reserved for special occasions. Incorporating touch into your daily routine, such as by holding hands or giving a hug when you see each other after a long day, can help to strengthen your connection.

Seek out touch-based activities: Engaging in touch-based activities, such as massages or couples' yoga, can be a fun and enjoyable way to strengthen your physical connection.

Practice good communication: Good communication is key to any healthy relationship, including in matters of physical affection. Make sure to discuss your desires, needs, and any concerns you may have with your partner.

Take breaks from technology: In today's digital age, it can be easy to get caught up in our screens and lose touch with our partners. Make an effort to take breaks from technology and focus on physical affection instead.

Practice touch in public: Physical affection doesn't have to be limited to private moments. Consider showing affection in public, such as by holding hands or giving a hug, to strengthen your connection and show your partner that you care.

Use touch to show affection and love: Physical affection is a powerful way to communicate love and affection to your partner. Make an effort to show your partner that you care through touch, such as by giving them a hug or a kiss.

Experiment with different types of touch: Touch can be a powerful way to communicate love and affection. Experiment with different types of touch, such as light or firm, and pay attention to your partner's responses to find out what they enjoy.

Make touch a priority: In today's busy world, it can be easy to let other commitments and responsibilities take precedence over your relationship. Make an effort to set aside quality time for each other and prioritize physical affection.

Practice touch during times of stress: Touch can be a powerful tool for reducing stress and promoting a sense of calm and connection. Consider using touch, such as holding hands or cuddling, during times of stress or anxiety to help alleviate tension and promote a sense of well-being.

Incorporate touch into your daily routine: Physical affection doesn't have to be reserved for special occasions. Incorporating touch into your daily routine, such as by holding hands or giving a hug when you see each other after a long day, can help to strengthen your connection.

Show your partner that you care: Physical affection is a powerful way to show your partner that you care about them and value your relationship. Make an effort to show your affection through touches, such as by giving them a hug or a kiss.

Experiment with different types of touch: Touch can be a powerful way to communicate love and affection. Experiment with different types of touch, such as light or firm, and pay attention to your partner's responses to find out what they enjoy.

Practice good communication: Good communication is key to any healthy relationship, including in matters of physical affection. Make sure to discuss your desires, needs, and any concerns you may have with your partner.

Remember, physical affection is an important aspect of any healthy relationship. By practicing touch during times of stress, incorporating touch into your daily routine, showing your partner that you care, experimenting with different types of touch, practicing good communication, taking breaks from technology, practicing touch in public, using touch to show affection and love, making touch a priority, practicing touch during the conflict, using touch to show appreciation and gratitude, incorporating touch into your daily routine, seeking out touch-based activities, and practicing good communication, you can strengthen your connection with your partner and improve overall relationship satisfaction.

CHAPTER NINE
EMBRACING VULNERABILITY AND AUTHENTICITY

Vulnerability and authenticity are important aspects of any healthy relationship, including in matters of sexuality. Allowing yourself to be vulnerable and authentic with your partner can help to build trust, deepen intimacy, and foster a more fulfilling sexual relationship.

Be open and honest about your thoughts and feelings: Allowing yourself to be vulnerable and authentic with your partner can help to build trust and deepen intimacy. No matter how difficult or uncomfortable your thoughts and feelings are, do not be discouraged to share them with your partner.

Seek out new experiences: Trying new things in the bedroom can help to keep things interesting and foster a sense of excitement and novelty. This can include things like introducing new positions, trying out different types of foreplay, or using toys or other enhancements.

Practice self-exploration: Engaging in self-exploration can help you gain a deeper understanding of your own desires and needs, which can in turn help you be more authentic and vulnerable with your partner.

Practice intimacy beyond the bedroom: Physical intimacy is an important aspect of any sexual relationship, but it is not the only aspect. Make an effort to connect emotionally and spiritually with your partner, both in and out of the bedroom.

Express your needs and desires: It is important to feel comfortable and safe expressing your needs and desires to your partner. Feel free to tell your partner your feelings no matter how difficult and uncomfortable your thoughts may be.

Seek to understand your partner's needs and desires: Understanding your partner's needs and desires can help to build trust and deepen intimacy. Make an effort to listen and ask your partner about their thoughts and feelings, and try to be open and understanding of their perspective.

Practice self-acceptance: In order to be vulnerable and authentic with your partner, it is important to first be accepting and loving towards yourself. Practice self-acceptance and self-compassion, and work on building a strong sense of self-worth.

Practice mindfulness: Being present and fully engaged in the moment can help to enhance the intimacy and pleasure of sexual activity. Consider incorporating mindfulness practices, such as meditation or focused breathing, into your sexual encounters.

Seek out activities that promote intimacy and connection: Engaging in activities that promote intimacy and connection, such as massages or couples' yoga, can be a fun and enjoyable way to strengthen your emotional and physical connection.

Make an effort to keep the romance alive: The romance and passion of a new relationship can fade over time, but it's important to make an effort to keep the spark alive in a long-term commitment. Try new things together, surprise each other, and keep the romance alive by doing things like planning special date nights and expressing your love and appreciation for one another.

Practice consent: Consent is an important aspect of any healthy sexual relationship. Make sure to communicate openly and honestly with your partner about your desires, boundaries, and limits, and respect their wishes as well.

Seek out activities that promote intimacy and connection: Engaging in activities that promote intimacy and connection, such as massages or couples' yoga, can be a fun and enjoyable way to strengthen your emotional and physical connection.

Practice intimacy beyond the bedroom: Physical intimacy is an important aspect of any sexual relationship, but it is not the only aspect. Make an effort to connect emotionally and spiritually with your partner, both in and out of the bedroom.

Practice mindfulness: Being present and fully engaged in the moment can help to enhance the intimacy and pleasure of sexual activity. Consider incorporating mindfulness practices, such as meditation or focused breathing, into your sexual encounters.

Seek out activities that promote intimacy and connection: Engaging in activities that promote intimacy and connection, such as massages or couples' yoga, can be a fun and enjoyable way to strengthen your emotional and physical connection.

Express your love and appreciation: Make an

effort to express your love and appreciation for your partner, both in and out of the bedroom. This can include things like telling them how much they mean to you, giving them a hug or a kiss, or simply saying "I love you."

Embracing vulnerability and authenticity in your sexual relationship requires effort and dedication, but the benefits can be significant. By practicing mindfulness, exploring fantasies and desires, practicing good communication, seeking out activities that promote intimacy and connection, making an effort to keep the romance alive, practicing intimacy beyond the bedroom, expressing your needs and desires, seeking to understand your partner's needs and desires, practicing self-acceptance, and seeking support if needed, you can build a more fulfilling and satisfying sexual relationship in your marriage.

CONCLUSION

The Joy of Sex in Marriage is a comprehensive guide to fostering deeper connection, intimacy, and pleasure in a committed relationship. By breaking the myth of the "normal" marriage and rejecting society's expectations, couples can prioritize their own pleasure and desires and openly communicate with one another about what they want and need in the bedroom. By exploring new sexual experiences and fantasies in a safe and consensual way, and by fostering emotional intimacy and connection, couples can reignite the passion and connection in their marriage. Navigating the challenges of long-term commitment and maintaining passion and connection over time can be difficult, but The Joy of Sex in Marriage offers practical strategies for doing so. By strengthening physical and emotional connection in daily life, understanding and prioritizing your own desires, using physical affection, and embracing vulnerability and authenticity, couples can revitalize their sexual relationship and enjoy a fulfilling, satisfying partnership.

A fulfilling and satisfying sexual relationship can be an important aspect of any healthy marriage. Maintaining passion and connection in your sexual relationship over the long term can be a challenge, but it is worth the effort. By keeping the romance alive, practicing good communication, and seeking out activities that promote intimacy and connection, you can strengthen your emotional and physical connection with your partner and improve overall relationship satisfaction.

It is also important to be open and honest with your partner about your thoughts and feelings, and to be open to trying new things and experimenting to find what works best for you as a couple. Practicing self-exploration and engaging in activities that promote intimacy and connection can also be

helpful in building a fulfilling sexual relationship.
With effort and dedication, you can build a fulfilling and satisfying sexual relationship in your marriage.

Ultimately, The Joy of Sex in Marriage is a valuable resource for any couple seeking to deepen their connection and intimacy in their committed relationship. Whether you are looking to reignite the spark in your marriage or simply want to explore new ways to connect with your partner, this book offers valuable insights and useful tips for partners. So, the joy of sex in marriage is a must-read for every couple who wants to strengthen their bond and relationship.
In summary, we provide a wealth of information and practical advice for couples looking to deepen their connection and intimacy in their committed relationships. By focusing on open and honest communication, exploring new sexual experiences and fantasies, and prioritizing emotional connection and vulnerability, couples can

reignite the passion and connection in their marriage and enjoy a fulfilling, satisfying partnership.

This book offers a wide range of strategies and techniques that couples can choose from to find what works best for them. It is also important to be patient and understanding with one another and to be willing to work together to overcome any challenges or difficulties that may arise.

Ultimately, The Joy of Sex in Marriage is a valuable resource for any couple seeking to strengthen their bond and deepen their connection in their committed relationship. Whether you are looking to reignite the spark in your marriage or simply want to explore new ways to connect with your partner, this book offers valuable insights and useful tips for couples irrespective of their ages. So, it is a must-read for every couple who wants to strengthen their bond and relationship.

It is important to remember that a fulfilling, satisfying sexual relationship in a marriage takes work and effort. It requires open and honest communication, a willingness to explore new experiences and fantasies, and a focus on emotional connection and vulnerability. However, the rewards of such a relationship are immeasurable. By following the guidance and advice offered in The Joy of Sex in Marriage, couples can deepen their connection and intimacy and enjoy a more fulfilling, satisfying partnership.

By breaking the myth of the "normal" marriage and rejecting society's expectations, couples can prioritize their own pleasure and desires and openly communicate with one another about what they want and need in the bedroom. By exploring new sexual experiences and fantasies in a safe and consensual way, and by fostering emotional intimacy and connection, couples can reignite the passion and connection in their marriage and enjoy a fulfilling, satisfying partnership.

HAPPINESS TO YOUR RELATIONSHIP

Printed in Great Britain
by Amazon